WHO JESUS IS

LifeChange

A NAVPRESS BIBLE STUDY SERIES

*A life-changing
encounter with God's Word*

WHO
JESUS IS

*Jesus' bold statements
of identity and relationship
can transform how we live.*

NavPress

A NavPress resource published in alliance
with Tyndale House Publishers

NavPress is the publishing ministry of The Navigators, an international Christian organization and leader in personal spiritual development. NavPress is committed to helping people grow spiritually and enjoy lives of meaning and hope through personal and group resources that are biblically rooted, culturally relevant, and highly practical.

For more information, visit NavPress.com.

Who Jesus Is: A Bible Study on the "I Am" Statements of Christ

Copyright © 2022 by The Navigators. All rights reserved.

A NavPress resource published in alliance with Tyndale House Publishers

NavPress and the NavPress logo are registered trademarks of NavPress, The Navigators, Colorado Springs, CO. *Tyndale* is a registered trademark of Tyndale House Ministries. Absence of ® in connection with marks of NavPress or other parties does not indicate an absence of registration of those marks.

Written by Jack Kuhatschek

The Team:
David Zimmerman, Publisher; Caitlyn Carlson, Editor; Elizabeth Schroll, Copy Editor; Olivia Eldredge, Operations Manager; Sarah Susan Richardson, Designer

Cover photograph of fabric texture copyright © Rawpixel. All rights reserved. Cover photograph of wood shavings copyright © simonkr/Getty Images. All rights reserved.

Author photo by Sandy Kuhatschek, 2016. All rights reserved.

All Scripture quotations, unless otherwise indicated, are taken from the Holy Bible, *New International Version,*® *NIV.*® Copyright © 1973, 1978, 1984, 2011 by Biblica, Inc.® Used by permission. All rights reserved worldwide. Scripture quotations marked ESV are from The ESV® Bible (The Holy Bible, English Standard Version®), copyright © 2001 by Crossway, a publishing ministry of Good News Publishers. Used by permission. All rights reserved. Scripture quotations marked NLT are taken from the *Holy Bible*, New Living Translation, copyright © 1996, 2004, 2015 by Tyndale House Foundation. Used by permission of Tyndale House Publishers, Carol Stream, Illinois 60188. All rights reserved.

Some of the anecdotal illustrations in this book are true to life and are included with the permission of the persons involved. All other illustrations are composites of real situations, and any resemblance to people living or dead is purely coincidental.

For information about special discounts for bulk purchases, please contact Tyndale House Publishers at csresponse@tyndale.com, or call 1-855-277-9400.

ISBN 978-1-64158-527-9

Printed in the United States of America

28	27	26	25	24	23	22
7	6	5	4	3	2	1

CONTENTS

HOW TO USE THIS STUDY

Objectives

The topical guides in the LifeChange series of Bible studies cover important topics from the Bible. Although the LifeChange guides vary with the topics they explore, they share some common goals:

1. to help readers grasp what key passages in the Bible say about the topic;

2. to provide readers with explanatory notes, word definitions, historical background, and cross-references so that the only other reference they need is the Bible;

3. to teach readers how to let God's Word transform them into Christ's image;

4. to provide small groups with a tool that will enhance group discussion of each passage and topic; and

5. to write each session so that advance preparation for group members is strongly encouraged but not required.

Each lesson in this study is designed to take forty-five minutes to complete.

Overview and Details

The study begins with an overview of the "I Am" statements of Jesus. The key to interpretation for each part of this study is content (what is the referenced passage *about*?), and the key to context is purpose (what is the author's *aim* for the passage as it relates to the overall topic?). Each lesson of the study explores one of the "I Am" statements of Jesus, with a corresponding passage from the Bible.

Kinds of Questions

Bible study provides different lenses and perspectives through which to engage the Scripture: observe (what does the passage *say*?), interpret (what does the passage *mean*?), and apply (how does this truth *affect* my life?). Some of the "how" and "why" questions will take some creative thinking, even prayer, to answer. Some are opinion questions without clear-cut right answers; these will lend themselves to discussions and side studies.

Don't let your study become an exercise in knowledge alone. Treat the passage as God's Word, and stay in dialogue with Him as you study. Pray, "Lord, what do You want me to see here?", "Father, why is this true?", and "Lord, how does this apply to my life?"

It is important that you write down your answers. The act of writing clarifies your thinking and helps you to remember what you're learning.

Study Aids

Throughout the guide, there are study aids that provide background information on the passage, insights from a commentary, or word studies. These aids are included in the guide to help you interpret the Bible without needing to use other, outside resources. Still, if you're interested in exploring further, the full resources are listed in the endnotes.

Scripture Versions

Unless otherwise indicated, the Bible quotations in this guide are from the New International Version of the Bible. Other versions cited are the English Standard Version and the New Living Translation.

Use any translation you like for study—or preferably more than one. Ideally you would have on hand a good, modern translation such as the New International Version, the English Standard Version, the New Living Translation, or the Christian Standard Bible. A paraphrase such as *The Message* is not accurate enough for study, but it can be helpful for comparison or devotional reading.

Memorizing and Meditating

A psalmist wrote, "I have hidden your word in my heart that I might not sin against you" (Psalm 119:11). If you write down a verse or passage that challenges or encourages you and reflect on it often for a week or more, you will find it beginning to affect your motives and actions. We forget quickly what we read once; we remember what we ponder.

When you find a significant verse or passage, you might copy it onto a card to keep with you. Set aside five minutes each day just to think about what the passage might mean in your life. Recite it to yourself, exploring its meaning. Then, return to the passage as often as you can during the day for a brief review. You will soon find it coming to mind spontaneously.

For Group Study

A group of four to ten people allows the richest discussions, but you can adapt this guide for other-sized groups. It will suit a wide range of group types, such as home Bible studies, growth groups, youth groups, and workplace Bible studies. Both new and experienced Bible students, and new and mature Christians, will benefit from the guide. You can omit or leave for later any questions you find too easy or too hard.

The guide is intended to lead a group through one lesson per meeting. This guide is formatted so you will be able to discuss each of the questions at length. Be sure to make time at each discussion for members to ask about anything they didn't understand.

Each member should prepare for a meeting by writing answers for all of the background and discussion questions to be covered. Application will be very difficult, however, without private thought and prayer.

Two reasons for studying in a group are accountability and support. When each member commits in front of the rest to seek growth in an area of life, you can pray for one another, listen jointly for God's guidance, help one another resist temptation, assure each other that each person's growth matters to you, use the group to practice spiritual principles, and so on. Pray about one another's commitments and needs at most meetings. If you wish, you can spend the first few minutes of each meeting sharing any results from applications prompted by previous lessons and discuss new applications toward the end of the meeting. Follow your time of sharing with prayer for these and other needs.

If you write down what others have shared, you are more likely to remember to pray for them during the week, ask about what they shared at the next meeting, and notice answered prayers. You might want to get a notebook for prayer requests and discussion notes.

Taking notes during discussion will help you remember to follow up on ideas, stay on the subject, and have clarity on an issue. But don't let note-taking keep you from participating.

Some best practices for groups:

1. If possible, come to the group discussion prepared. The more each group member knows about the passage and the questions being asked, the better your discussion will be.

2. Realize that the group leader will not be teaching from the passage but instead will be facilitating your discussion. Therefore, it is important for each group member to participate so that everyone can contribute to what you learn as a group.

3. Try to stick to the passage covered in the session and the specific questions in the study guide.

4. Listen attentively to the other members of the group when they are sharing their thoughts about the passage. Also, realize that most of the questions are open-ended, allowing for more than one answer.

5. Be careful not to dominate the discussion—especially if you are the leader. Allow time for everyone to share their thoughts and ideas.

6. As mentioned previously, throughout the session are study aids that provide background information on the passage, insights from a commentary, or word studies. Reading these aloud during the meeting is optional and up to the discussion leader. However, each member can refer to these insights if they found them helpful in understanding the passage.

A Note on Topical Studies

LifeChange guides offer a robust and thoughtful engagement with God's Word. The book-centric guides focus on a step-by-step walk through that particular book of the Bible. The topical studies use Scripture to help you engage more deeply with God's Word and its implications for your life.

INTRODUCTION

Who Jesus Is

WHO IS JESUS? Ask any number of people, and you'll get any number of answers. Was He the greatest teacher who ever lived? A wonderful moral example? A prophet? God?

Many people put their own spin on the person of Jesus. Some view Him as a failed prophet whose movement outlived Him. Others suggest that Jesus was simply a philosopher, a teacher of wisdom in the Cynic tradition (meaning he "renounced worldly goods and social conventions"). Still others believe He was simply a revolutionary who was influenced by the Zealot movement.[1]

But very few people try to argue that He wasn't a real person—and that's because we have access to vivid detail we don't get about many historical figures: extensive accounts about Jesus' life and ministry in the four biblical Gospels (Matthew, Mark, Luke, and John). People who walked with Jesus (Matthew and John) or people who knew those who walked with Jesus (Mark and Luke) carefully wrote down what they considered most important about Him—not just events but things He said— and the Gospels as a whole paint a remarkably consistent picture. The reality is, when we don't take the Gospels into account in our understanding of Jesus, our views of Jesus end up reflecting who we want Him to be, not who He really is. And when we take Jesus at His word, we see that He was far more than just a prophet or a teacher.

The Gospels paint a picture not just of the life of Jesus—from his geneaology, to his birth, to his life and death—but zoom in to give us His very words, the things He considered most important to pass along during His time on earth. The Gospel of John shows us a series of extraordinary claims Jesus made about who He is and why He came.

In this LifeChange study guide, we will look at eight amazing "I Am" statements Jesus made about Himself. Each session in the guide will focus on a key passage of Scripture that explores one "I Am" statement and its context. There will also be suggestions at the end of each session for studying related passages.

Jesus wants every Christian to know who He is and what He has done for us. This LifeChange guide will lead you through what Jesus has said about Himself, revealing that the Messiah and Savior is far greater and more powerful than anyone could have imagined.

I AM THE BREAD OF LIFE

John 6:25-59

IS THERE ANYTHING BETTER than fresh-baked bread? When I was in elementary school, we went on a field trip in Dallas to the headquarters and factory of Mrs. Baird's, a bakery known for its bread. After we watched the dough being poured into pans on an assembly line and then cooked in an oven, we were each given a small, fresh-baked loaf of bread that was still warm and covered with butter. We all thought it was the best bread we had ever eaten!

In our day, bread is often an optional part of a meal. But in Jesus' day, bread was the most significant part of the meal and the primary means for satisfying people's daily hunger. In a very real sense, their lives depended on bread. In this passage, which follows the feeding of the five thousand, Jesus claims to be the Bread of Life—spiritual sustenance that enables those who eat it to live forever!

1. Read John 6:25-59. Which of Jesus' statements stands out to you most? Why?

_____

_____

_____

_____

_____

_____

_____

2. Read John 6:12-15, 23-24. Who was looking for Jesus? Why were they looking for Him?

_____

_____

_____

_____

_____

_____

_____

_____

_____

_____

_____

3. How does Jesus expose and redirect the crowd's misguided motive (see verses 25-29)?

_____

_____

_____

_____

_____

_____

_____

_____

_____

_____

_____

4. What is ironic about the crowd's request for a "sign" like their ancestors received in the wilderness (see verses 30-31)?

_____

_____

_____

_____

_____

_____

_____

_____

_____

Gary Burge writes: "Judaism understood that there was a storehouse or 'treasury' of manna in heaven that had been opened to feed the people during the era of Moses. The Israelites had been fed with 'bread from heaven.' This treasury would be reopened with the coming of the Messiah: 'The treasury of manna shall again descend from on high, and they will eat of it in those years' (2 Bar. 29:8). . . . An early Jewish commentary on Exodus 16:4 says, 'As the first redeemer caused manna to descend . . . so will the *latter redeemer* cause manna to descend' (*Midrash Rabbah Eccles.* 1:9)."[1]

5. How do verses 32-34 underscore the crowd's confusion about what Jesus is saying?

_____

_____

_____

_____

_____

_____

_____

_____

_____

_____

_____

_____

_____

"Jesus is 'living bread,' as once before he offered 'living water.' This famous saying ('I am the bread of life') heads the list of what we call the 'I-am sayings' in John. . . .

"In each of these sayings Jesus is taking a motif from Judaism (often in the context of a miracle or major festival discourse) and reinterpreting it for himself."[2]

6. How does Jesus explain his claim, "I am the bread of life. Whoever comes to me will never go hungry, and whoever believes in me will never be thirsty" (verse 35; see verses 35-40)?

_____

_____

_____

_____

_____

_____

_____

_____

_____

7. Our spiritual hunger and thirst will not be fully satisfied until our resurrection in the new heaven and earth. But how has Jesus already begun to satisfy your spiritual needs?

_____

_____

_____

_____

_____

_____

_____

_____

_____

_____

_____

8. What reasons do the Jews give for rejecting Jesus' extravagant claims (see verses 41-42)?

_____

_____

_____

_____

_____

_____

_____

_____

_____

_____

_____

9. Instead of answering their question at the end of verse 42, Jesus focuses on the real reason why they fail to understand him. What explanation does He give in verses 44-50?

_____

_____

_____

_____

_____

_____

_____

_____

_____

_____

_____

_____

Gary Burge explains: "The idea of Jesus' divine origin and descent (supplied to us as readers in ch. 1) is impossible for the crowd unless God in some fashion illumines them. John 6:44 parallels 6:37 (emphasizing God's sovereignty) but now is followed by an explanation of what this 'drawing' means. John 6:45 echoes Isaiah 54:13 (or Jer. 31:33-34), where the prophet foresees a rebuilt Jerusalem (following the Exile) where intimacy with God will be regained. Jesus looks at this prophesy and sees its relevance. God must move the inner heart of a person before he or she can see the things of God. And this takes place on God's initiative (cf. 5:37)."[3]

Some scholars believe that Jesus is speaking of the Eucharist or "Lord's Supper," where Christians partake of the bread and wine. But that sacrament is a symbolic reminder that those who believe in Jesus partake of the benefits of His literal broken body and shed blood on the cross.

10. Jesus alienates many in the crowd when He tells them, "Unless you eat the flesh of the Son of Man and drink his blood, you have no life in you" (verse 53). To them it sounds like cannibalism. What do you think He means by this radical statement, and why do you think he gave it?

_____

_____

_____

_____

_____

_____

_____

_____

_____

_____

11. Understanding who Jesus is should affect how we follow Him. How do Jesus' words "I am the bread of life" (verse 35) equip you to do what He has called you to do?

_____

_____

_____

_____

_____

_____

_____

_____

_____

_____

Your Response

We are all looking for something to fill what is empty within us. Who do you know who needs "the Bread of Life"?

_____

_____

_____

_____

_____

_____

_____

_____

_____

_____

_____

_____

_____

_____

_____

_____

_____

_____

_____

_____

_____

_____

For Further Study

Read Exodus 16, which describes the "bread from heaven" (manna) that the Lord gave to the Israelites during the Exodus. How does their grumbling foreshadow the grumbling of those who heard Jesus in John 6:25-59?

_____

_____

_____

_____

_____

_____

_____

_____

_____

_____

_____

_____

_____

_____

_____

_____

_____

_____

_____

_____

_____

I AM THE LIGHT OF THE WORLD

John 9

In 2003 CONNIE PARKE'S VISION in both eyes got so bad that she couldn't work or drive. An eye doctor told her she had detached retinas and there was nothing he could do. "I pretty much stopped going to doctors at that point," Parke said. She enrolled in a school for the blind in Denver and learned how to use a cane and read Braille. But after fifteen years of legal blindness, Parke was encouraged to visit Dr. Jeffrey SooHoo, an associate professor in the ophthalmology department at the University of Colorado School of Medicine. He examined her eyes and determined that her problem was not detached retinas but rather cataracts. After her first short surgery, Parke was speechless and began to cry. She now had 20/20 vision![1]

Today, blindness makes the everyday rhythms of life more difficult, and having sight restored can be an extraordinary gift. But in Jesus' day, blindness prevented people from meeting their own basic needs. Blind people struggled to survive, and many became beggars.[2] Sight would be not only life-changing but also life-saving. In John 9, Jesus gives sight to a man born blind, proving His claim that He is the Light of the World by illuminating darkness not just physically but spiritually.

1. Read John 9. What statements and reactions stand out to you? Why?

_____

_____

_____

_____

_____

_____

_____

_____

_____

_____

2. What are the different ways in which people describe Jesus throughout this passage?

_____

_____

_____

_____

_____

_____

D. A. Carson writes: "The disciples assume, like most Palestinian Jews of their day, that sin and suffering are intimately connected. In one sense, they are correct; they are simply working out the entailments of the fall (Gn. 3). . . . But once theologians move from generalizing statements about the origin of the human race's maladies to tight connections between the sins and the sufferings of *an individual*, they go beyond the biblical evidence (whether from the Old Testament or the New)."[3]

3. How does Jesus refute the disciples' false assumption that the man's blindness was due to sin (see verses 1-3)?

_____

_____

_____

_____

_____

_____

_____

_____

_____

_____

4. What do you think Jesus means when He refers to "day," "night," and "I am the light of the world" (see verses 4-5)?

_____

_____

_____

_____

_____

_____

_____

_____

_____

_____

5. When Jesus heals the blind man (see verses 6-7), what does that demonstrate about Jesus' claim in verse 5 and the condition of humanity?

_____

_____

_____

_____

_____

_____

_____

_____

_____

_____

_____

6. John describes four scenes where questions are discussed. What does each scene reveal about the man's increasing spiritual sight and the Pharisees' spiritual blindness?

the man and his neighbors (see verses 8-12):

_____

_____

_____

_____

_____

_____

_____

_____

_____

_____

the Pharisees and the man (see verses 13-17):

_____

_____

_____

_____

_____

_____

_____

_____

_____

_____

_____

_____

_____

the Pharisees and the man's parents (see verses 18-23):

_____

_____

_____

_____

_____

_____

_____

_____

_____

_____

the Pharisees and the man (see verses 24-34):

_____

_____

_____

_____

_____

_____

_____

_____

_____

_____

"Each of these scenes probes the identity of Jesus, and each betrays a deeper literary function. As the story progresses, Jesus is more closely revealed by name: He is 'Jesus' (9:10), then he is called a 'prophet' (9:17), then 'the Christ' (9:22), and finally, he is declared to be 'from God' (9:33). It is easy to see the Christological progression of each name as the story develops. While the Pharisees repudiate Jesus and his role, the discussion drives home his true identity."[4]

7. Describe your personal journey from spiritual darkness to the light of Jesus Christ.

_____

_____

_____

_____

_____

_____

_____

_____

_____

_____

_____

8. In verse 35, Jesus asks the man, "Do you believe in the Son of Man?" What do you learn about the Son of Man from Daniel 7:13-14?

_____

_____

_____

_____

_____

_____

_____

_____

_____

_____

_____

_____

9. What do you think Jesus means when He says, "For judgment I have come into this world, so that the blind will see and those who see will become blind" (verse 39)?

_____

_____

_____

_____

_____

_____

_____

_____

_____

10. Jesus tells the Pharisees, "Now that you claim you can see, your guilt remains" (verse 41). We cannot claim to see when we are in complete darkness. How does believing Jesus' statement that He is the Light of the World move us from "claiming to see" to actually being able to see?

_____

_____

_____

_____

_____

What is it that we now see, in the light of who He is?

_____

_____

_____

_____

_____

Your Response

The formerly blind man declared his faith even in the face of opposition. What would it look like for you to speak more boldly about what Jesus has done?

_____

_____

_____

_____

_____

_____

_____

_____

_____

_____

_____

_____

_____

_____

_____

_____

_____

_____

_____

_____

_____

_____

_____

_____

_____

For Further Study

Read John 8:12-20. What more can you learn about Jesus being the Light of the World from this passage?

_____

_____

_____

_____

_____

_____

_____

_____

Next read Revelation 21:22-27. What does it say about the Lamb?

_____

_____

_____

_____

_____

_____

_____

_____

_____

I AM THE GATE FOR THE SHEEP

John 10:1-10

A FEW YEARS AGO, a friend of mine invited me to join him and twenty-five others on a tour of Israel. On one of our first stops, we visited a sheep pen. I'd always imagined these enclosures made of either wood or metal. But in Israel the most common material is stone, and therefore the enclosure we saw was made of large rocks piled on top of each other to a height of about three feet.

This is the type of pen that Jesus' readers would have seen in first-century Israel. There was only one gate into the sheep pen, and a watchman, who was a hired hand, only allowed certain shepherds and sheep to enter that gate. In smaller sheep pens, the shepherd himself would sometimes lie down at the entrance to the pen, becoming a human gate that protected the sheep from all intruders. In John 10 Jesus tells the Pharisees that He is the gate into the sheep pen.[1]

1. Read John 10:1-10. What key words and phrases jump out at you? Why?

_____

_____

_____

_____

_____

_____

D. A. Carson writes: "The details would be familiar to John's readers. The sheep are in a fold, a sheep pen. This might be part of a family courtyard; in view of v. 3, it is better to think of a larger, independent enclosure, where several families kept their sheep, hiring an undershepherd (the 'watchman' of v. 2) to guard the gate. Those who were authorized to enter would of course do so through the gate. He whose interest is stealing or wounding the sheep would avoid the gate; he *climbs in by some other way.*"[2]

2. What do you notice about how Jesus approaches
His interaction with the Pharisees?

_____

_____

_____

_____

_____

_____

_____

_____

_____

_____

In these verses, Jesus talks about shepherds,
sheep, and the gate to the sheepfold. However, as
He speaks directly to the Pharisees, He focuses on
thieves and robbers (verse 1). Why might He have
done this (see Ezekiel 34:1-6)?

_____

_____

_____

_____

_____

_____

_____

_____

_____

_____

3. What kind of relationship does the true shepherd have with his sheep (see verses 2-4)?

_____

_____

_____

_____

_____

How is this similar to the purpose of the gate?

_____

_____

_____

_____

_____

"Unlike Western shepherds who drive the sheep, often using a sheep dog, the shepherds of the Near East, both now and in Jesus' day, lead their flocks, their voice calling them on. That such a shepherd goes ahead of his sheep and draws them constitutes an admirable picture of the master/disciple relationship. The sheep follow simply *because they know his voice*; by the same token, they will run from anyone else because *they do not recognise a stranger's voice.*"[3]

4. What kinds of false shepherds try to plunder Jesus' followers today, and how can we guard ourselves against them?

_____

_____

_____

_____

_____

_____

_____

_____

D. A. Carson explains: "Jesus' opponents *did not understand what he was telling them*. How could they? They were not of his sheep (*cf.* v. 26). And when they do begin to grasp what he says, their limited understanding only serves as the basis for rejecting him (*e.g.* 5:16ff.; 6:60; 7:20, 45ff.; 8:31ff.; 9:39-41). John's comment in this verse is therefore simultaneously a theological indictment and a step toward the further explanations in the next verses. Misunderstanding is frequently followed by explication in this Gospel."[4]

5. Why do you think the Pharisees, who were experts in the Old Testament, did not understand what Jesus was telling them (see verse 6)?

_____

_____

_____

_____

_____

_____

_____

_____

_____

_____

6. What parallels do you see between verses 7-9 and John 14:6?

_____

_____

_____

_____

_____

_____

_____

_____

_____

_____

_____

_____

7. The second half of verse 10 has been translated a variety of ways. How do each of the following translations enhance your understanding of what Jesus is saying?

"I have come that they may have life, and have it to the full" (NIV):

_____

_____

_____

_____

_____

_____

_____

_____

"My purpose is to give them a rich and satisfying life" (NLT):

_____

_____

_____

_____

_____

_____

_____

_____

_____

_____

_____

"I came that they may have life and have it
abundantly" (ESV):

_____

_____

_____

_____

_____

_____

_____

_____

_____

_____

8. Although Jesus' promise will not be completely
fulfilled until He returns, in what ways have you
experienced a richer, fuller life as a Christian?

_____

_____

_____

_____

_____

_____

_____

_____

_____

_____

_____

9. How does Jesus' promise motivate you to share the good news with others?

_____

_____

_____

_____

_____

_____

_____

_____

_____

_____

10. How does the picture of Jesus as the Gate for the sheep help us understand the abundant life He offers (see verses 9-10)?

_____

_____

_____

_____

_____

_____

_____

_____

_____

_____

_____

_____

Your Response

In what ways do you seek to hear Jesus' voice today?

_____

_____

_____

_____

_____

_____

_____

_____

_____

_____

_____

_____

_____

_____

_____

_____

_____

_____

_____

_____

_____

_____

_____

_____

_____

For Further Study

Read Ezekiel 34:1-16. How does this passage explain why Jesus viewed the so-called shepherds of Israel as thieves and robbers?

_____

_____

_____

_____

_____

_____

_____

_____

_____

_____

_____

_____

_____

_____

_____

_____

_____

_____

_____

_____

_____

_____

_____

_____

I AM THE GOOD SHEPHERD

John 10:11-21

WE ARE INSPIRED by acts of heroism and bravery, especially when they involve the ultimate sacrifice: a soldier who pushed a young girl out of the way of a military truck only to be struck and killed himself; the passengers on the *Titanic* who gave their life jackets to others; the man who survived the crash of Air Florida Flight 90 but repeatedly handed the helicopter lifelines to others, even though it meant he would not be rescued himself.

In Jesus' day, shepherds often faced danger—they were charged with protecting the sheep from wild animals and thieves, after all. But in John 10, Jesus goes far beyond the usual standards of a shepherd's protection: He says that as the Good Shepherd, He lays down His own life to save His sheep.

1. Read John 10:11-21. What repeated words or phrases do you notice?

_____

_____

_____

_____

_____

_____

_____

_____

"Jesus claims that he is the 'good shepherd' (10:11-18). It is important not to overly sentimentalize the image given here. This is not a portrait of a kindly man holding cuddly lambs. 'Good' (Gk. *kalos*) can just as well be translated 'noble.' The shepherd's job was severe, tiring, and hazardous."[1]

2. Jesus calls Himself "the good shepherd" three times in this passage. In what ways does the good shepherd differ from the hired hand (see verses 11-13)?

_____

_____

_____

_____

_____

_____

_____

_____

_____

_____

3. Jesus says that the Good Shepherd lays down his life "for the sheep" (verse 11). In John's Gospel the word *for* (*hyper* in the Greek) is always used in a sacrificial context (see John 6:51, 10:15, 11:50-52, 17:19, and 18:14).[2] How does this clarify Jesus' purpose in going to the cross?

_____

_____

_____

_____

_____

_____

_____

_____

_____

_____

4. In what sense is Jesus' relationship with His sheep like His relationship with the Father—and why is this significant for us (see verses 14-15)?

_____

_____

_____

_____

_____

_____

_____

_____

_____

_____

5. In your opinion, who are the "other sheep" that are "not of this sheep pen" but will become part of one flock with one shepherd (see verse 16)?

_____

_____

_____

_____

_____

_____

_____

_____

_____

_____

_____

6. God's family is multinational and multiethnic—
"sheep that are not of [our] sheep pen," or people
who are not from our racial, social, or national
context. How should this reality affect the way we
relate to, listen to, and learn from our brothers
and sisters in Christ?

_____

_____

_____

_____

_____

_____

_____

_____

_____

Gary Burge explains that
Jesus' death "is not merely
about obedience to God
nor is it his personal honor.
Rather, Jesus is willing to
die because of his profound
commitment to the ones
he loves. As Paul writes,
'Christ loved the church and
gave himself up for her . . .
to present her to himself as
a radiant church, without
stain or wrinkle or any
other blemish, but holy and
blameless' (Eph. 5:25, 27)."[4]

7. Some have referred to Jesus' death as "cosmic
child abuse,"[3] where the Father forces His Son to
die for our sins. How does Jesus dispel that myth
in verses 17-18?

_____

_____

_____

_____

_____

_____

_____

_____

_____

_____

8. Jesus explains that He has the authority to lay down His life and to take it up again (verse 18). How would Jesus' death be meaningless apart from the resurrection (see 1 Corinthians 15:12-19)?

_____

_____

_____

_____

_____

_____

_____

_____

_____

D. A. Carson writes: "Jesus lays down his life *in order to* take it up again. Jesus' sacrificial death was not an end in itself, and his resurrection an afterthought. His death was with the resurrection in view. He died in order to rise, and by his rising to proceed toward his ultimate glorification (12:23; 17:5) and the pouring out of the Spirit (7:37-39) so that others, too, might live."[5]

9. John tells us that those who heard Jesus that day were divided (see verse 19). How does their response resemble those who hear the gospel today (seeverses 19-21)?

_____

_____

_____

_____

_____

_____

_____

_____

_____

_____

_____

10. How does your understanding of the Good
Shepherd help you understand the heart of Jesus?

_____

_____

_____

_____

_____

_____

_____

_____

_____

_____

Your Response

Reread what Jesus says in this passage about how
He cares for the sheep. How does this motivate
you to follow Him?

_____

_____

_____

_____

_____

_____

_____

_____

_____

_____

_____

For Further Study

Read Psalm 23, and reflect on what it means to have the Lord as your shepherd.

I AM THE RESURRECTION AND THE LIFE

John 11:1-44

D. L. MOODY, a famous evangelist from the Victorian era, once said, "Some day you will read in the papers, 'D. L. Moody of East Northfield is dead.' Don't you believe a word of it! At that moment I shall be more alive than I am now."[1]

Resurrection is the foundation of our faith. But resurrection is more than a past event or a future hope; it is a person. Our hope, like Moody's, is grounded in the promise of Jesus' words in John 11:25-26: "I am the resurrection and the life. The one who believes in me will live, even though they die; and whoever lives by believing in me will never die."

---

1. Read John 11:1-44. What key words or phrases give insight into Jesus' relationship with Martha, Mary, and Lazarus?

_____

_____

_____

_____

_____

_____

_____

_____

2. What statements in this passage seem most significant to you?

_____

_____

_____

_____

Which ones surprise you?

_____

_____

_____

_____

_____

Gary Burge writes: "When Jesus finally arrives in Bethany Lazarus has been dead for four days. This note is significant. There was a well-known Jewish belief (attested from about A.D. 200) that the soul of a dead person remained in the vicinity of the body 'hoping to reenter it' for three days, but once decomposition set in, the soul departed. John wants us to know clearly that Lazarus is truly dead and that the miracle of Jesus cannot be construed as a resuscitation."[2]

3. How do verses 7-16 clarify the seeming contradiction between verses 5 and 6?

_____

_____

_____

_____

_____

_____

_____

_____

_____

_____

4. How does Martha exhibit both faith and a misunderstanding of what Jesus promises (see verses 17-24)?

_____

_____

_____

_____

_____

_____

_____

_____

_____

5. Jesus is making two separate but related claims in verses 25-26. How would you explain each claim's meaning?

"I am the resurrection. . . . The one who believes in me will live, even though they die."

_____

_____

_____

_____

_____

_____

_____

_____

_____

_____

Jesus' "correction leads to one of the most famous and significant 'I am' sayings in John's Gospel. Jesus does not say that he can provide resurrection and life (though this is implicit). That in itself would be astounding. In fact, the Synoptics recount stories of Jesus' authority over death and his ability to call someone back to life (e.g., the widow's son in Nain in Luke 7:11-17; Jairus's daughter in Mark 5:21-43). But Jesus says that *he is* resurrection and life."[3]

The Greek word *anastasis* (resurrection) means "a rising from the dead."[4] The word is used in the New Testament to speak of both the resurrection of Christ and the resurrection of all humanity at the end of this present age. The word *zōē* (life) can refer to both literal and figurative life.[5] The power over death, physical life, and the fullness of existence all emerge from who Jesus is.

"I am . . . the life. . . . Whoever lives by believing in me will never die."

_____

_____

_____

_____

_____

_____

_____

_____

_____

_____

_____

6. How do Jesus' claims in verses 25-26 give you comfort and hope?

_____

_____

_____

_____

_____

_____

_____

_____

_____

_____

_____

7. What does Mary's visit with Jesus reveal about His heart (see verses 28-37)?

_____

_____

_____

_____

_____

_____

_____

_____

_____

_____

8. What do you think went through the minds of Mary, Martha, and their friends as the scene unfolds in verses 38-44?

_____

_____

_____

_____

_____

_____

_____

_____

_____

_____

_____

_____

9. How does the statement "I am the resurrection and the life" help you understand the bigger picture of who Jesus is?

_____

_____

_____

_____

_____

_____

_____

_____

Your Response

How does this entire passage reveal "the glory of God" (verse 40) in the face of Jesus Christ?

_____

_____

_____

_____

_____

How does our belief in the work of Jesus reveal the glory of God?

_____

_____

_____

_____

_____

_____

For Further Study

Read 1 Corinthians 15:12-58. How does this passage help you understand the future resurrection of those who believe in Jesus?

_____

_____

_____

_____

_____

_____

_____

_____

_____

_____

_____

_____

_____

_____

_____

_____

_____

_____

_____

_____

_____

_____

I AM THE WAY, THE TRUTH, AND THE LIFE

John 14:1-14

CHRISTIANS ARE OFTEN CRITICIZED for claiming that Jesus is the only way to God. After all, there are billions of non-Christians in the world. Are we really so narrow-minded that we think these people will be excluded from heaven just because they happened to have been taught the wrong religion? Rabbi Schmuley Boteach summed up the feelings of many when he said, "I am absolutely against any religion that says that one faith is superior to another. I don't see how that is anything different than spiritual racism."[1]

Yet, as we will see in this passage, Christians are not the ones who originally made this claim. Instead, it was Jesus Himself who proclaimed, "I am the way and the truth and the life. No one comes to the Father except through me" (verse 6). Jesus is not excluding anyone from His offer of salvation. But He clearly teaches that we cannot be saved apart from Him, and we are given the choice whether we will accept or reject His gift of life. The reality is that none of us have any way to God on our own, and no other religion or spirituality of this world can create one for us. Jesus steps into our need and offers us Himself as the only true path to God.

---

1. Read John 14:1-14. What might be some of the reasons why the disciples' hearts are troubled (see John 13:21, 33, 38)?

   _____

   _____

   _____

_____

_____

_____

_____

_____

2. What do you observe about the relationship between the Father and the Son in this passage?

_____

_____

_____

_____

_____

_____

_____

"The Greek word *monē*, cognate with the verb *menō* ('to remain', 'to stay', 'to dwell'), properly signifies a 'dwelling place'. Because the Latin Vulgate rendered it *mansiones*, the AV/KJV, followed by the RV, used 'mansions'. However, since heaven is here pictured as the Father's *house*, it is more natural to think of 'dwelling-places' within a house as *rooms* (NIV) or suites or the like."[2]

3. How would Jesus' words in 14:1-3 comfort and strengthen the disciples?

_____

_____

_____

_____

_____

_____

_____

_____

_____

_____

4. In response to what Jesus said in verse 4, Thomas protests, "Lord, we don't know where you are going, so how can we know the way?" (verse 5). How is Jesus' answer radically different from saying, "I *show* you the way; I *teach* you the truth, and I *offer* you life"?

_____

_____

_____

_____

_____

_____

_____

_____

_____

_____

5. How would you respond to someone who struggled with Jesus' claim that "No one comes to the Father except through me" (verse 6)?

_____

_____

_____

_____

_____

_____

_____

_____

_____

_____

"If Jesus is, in fact, God himself, that puts his claim in an entirely different light. An infinite being can say with certainty whether there is one God or many, and whether there are multiple ways to know him or only one. Jesus doesn't say that he merely speaks the truth; he claims to be the embodiment of Truth. He doesn't say he can give life; he tells us he is the source of life itself. And he doesn't say he is one pathway to God among many; he asserts that he is the only Way."[3]

6. How does Jesus explain what He means when He says, "Anyone who has seen me has seen the Father" (verse 9; see verses 7-11)?

_____

_____

_____

_____

_____

_____

_____

_____

_____

_____

"The NIV indicates an interesting variation in 1:18: 'No one has ever seen God, but *God* the One and Only, who is at the Father's side, has made him known.' Some manuscripts insert 'Son' for 'God,' but the NIV's more difficult, explicit affirmation of Christ's divinity is likely original. John 1:18 then joins 1:1 as the closing frame of the prologue, offering a summary statement about the divine origin and exhaustive knowledge of the Son. Christ's revelation is unique for ontological reasons: It is his identity, his being, the essence of who he is that makes his words God's words. Indeed, Christ is fully God, who in his incarnation is revealing *himself* to the world."[4]

7. How do verses 7-11 reinforce what John said at the beginning of his Gospel (1:1-5, 9-13, 18)?

_____

_____

_____

_____

_____

_____

_____

_____

_____

_____

_____

_____

8. Jesus makes the startling claim that "Whoever believes in me . . . will do even greater things" than He has done (verse 12). What does Jesus mean, and how is this possible (see verses 13-14; see also verses 15-17)?

_____

_____

_____

_____

_____

_____

_____

_____

_____

Leon Morris writes: "What Jesus means we may see in the narratives of the Acts. There there are a few miracles of healing, but the emphasis is on the mighty works of conversion. On the day of Pentecost alone more believers were added to the little band of believers than throughout Christ's entire earthly life. There we see a literal fulfillment of 'greater works than these shall he do.'"[5]

9. In what ways is the church today doing the works that Jesus did while He was here on earth?

_____

_____

_____

_____

_____

_____

_____

_____

_____

_____

_____

10. This is the beauty of the gospel: that God, knowing that our sin would keep us forever separated from Him, came to earth in the person of Jesus to become the Way back into relationship. How does the abundance of the good news stand in contrast to the assertion that Christianity is narrow-minded?

_____

_____

_____

_____

_____

_____

_____

_____

_____

Your Response

Since Jesus is the only way to God, how does that make the Great Commission (Matthew 28:18-20) vitally important?

_____

_____

_____

_____

_____

_____

_____

_____

How does Jesus' promise, "I will do whatever you ask in my name, so that the Father may be glorified in the Son" (John 14:13) motivate you to pray?

_____

_____

_____

_____

_____

_____

_____

_____

_____

_____

_____

_____

_____

_____

_____

_____

_____

_____

_____

_____

_____

_____

_____

_____

For Further Study

Read the following meditation of Thomas à Kempis:

Follow thou me. I am the way and the truth
and the life. Without the way there is no
going; without the truth there is no knowing;
without the life there is no living. I am the
way which thou must follow; the truth which
thou must believe; the life for which thou
must hope. I am the inviolable way; the
infallible truth, the never-ending life. I am
the straightest way; the sovereign truth; life
true, life blessed, life uncreated.[6]

What insight about Jesus from this meditation
resonates most with you? Why?

_____

_____

_____

_____

_____

_____

_____

_____

_____

_____

_____

_____

_____

_____

_____

_____

_____

_____

I AM THE TRUE VINE

John 15:1-17

A FEW YEARS AGO, my wife and I toured several vineyards in northern Michigan. We normally associate vineyards with France, Italy, or California, but Michigan wines are growing in popularity. We visited Chateau Grand Traverse, Chateau Chantal, Bowers Harbor Vineyards, and several others. The common feature at each vineyard was row after row of lush vines loaded with grapes.

We know intuitively that vines loaded with grapes are healthy, producing and thriving in the ways they are meant to. That's why the vine is such a vivid metaphor in Scripture, used to help us understand the source and the fruit of the abundant life. In the Old Testament, Israel is described as a vine planted and cultivated by the Lord that did not bear fruit (see, for example, Isaiah 5:1-7). But in John 15, Jesus claims to be "the true vine," and says branches that "remain in [Him] . . . bear much fruit" (John 15:1, 5).

1. Read John 15:1-17. What key words and phrases do you see repeated?

---

2. What is the role of the vine?

_____

_____

_____

_____

_____

What is the role of the branches?

_____

_____

_____

_____

_____

Andreas Köstenberger writes: "References to Israel as God's vine regularly stress Israel's failure to produce good fruit, issuing in divine judgment. . . . In contrast to Israel's failure, Jesus claims to be the 'true vine,' bringing forth the fruit that Israel failed to produce. Thus Jesus, the Messiah and Son of God, fulfills Israel's destiny as the true vine of God (Ps. 80:14-17)."[1]

3. In what sense is Jesus the "true vine" in contrast to Israel?

_____

_____

_____

_____

_____

_____

_____

_____

_____

_____

_____

_____

4. How does the Father tend to the branches that bear fruit (see verses 1-4)?

_____

_____

_____

_____

_____

_____

_____

_____

_____

_____

_____

5. How does Jesus contrast those branches that remain in him with those that do not (see verses 5-6)?

_____

_____

_____

_____

_____

_____

_____

_____

_____

_____

_____

All of the "I am" statements in John's Gospel emphasize that Jesus alone is the source of eternal life, and only those who believe in Him and follow Him receive that life. But as the parable of the sower demonstrates (Matthew 13:1-23), not all who initially profess faith in Jesus are his true disciples. Instead, some "fall away" from him and therefore cannot bear fruit (Matthew 13:21). In contrast, those who remain in Jesus are connected to him as the life-giving vine and will be pruned and cared for in order to "bear much fruit" (John 15:5).

6. According to Jesus, how is our fruit-bearing related to prayer (see verses 7-8)?

_____

_____

_____

_____

In what ways have you seen the relationship between prayer and fruit in your own life?

_____

_____

_____

_____

7. In verses 9-11, Jesus drops the vine imagery and speaks more plainly to His disciples. How do you respond to the statement that Jesus' love for you is as great as the Father's love for Jesus (see verses 9 and 11)?

_____

_____

_____

_____

_____

_____

_____

_____

_____

_____

8. Jesus mentions keeping His "commands" (plural) in verse 10 and his "command" (singular) in verse 12. How are these closely related (see Matthew 22:34-40)?

_____

_____

_____

_____

_____

_____

_____

_____

_____

_____

When Jesus says, "If you keep my commands, you will remain in my love" (verse 10), it sounds as though Christ's love is conditional on our obedience instead of our obedience being a response to his love. But in John's first epistle, he clarifies that both obedience and love are like vital signs that demonstrate that we are truly alive in Christ, and those who lack those vital signs are not true believers. John writes, "We know that we have come to know him if we keep his commands. Whoever says, 'I know him,' but does not do what he commands is a liar, and the truth is not in that person" (1 John 2:3-4), and, "We know that we have passed from death to life, because we love each other. Anyone who does not love remains in death" (1 John 3:14).

9. Jesus tells us in verse 13: "Greater love has no one than this: to lay down one's life for one's friends." What are some tangible ways you can sacrificially love and serve others in your daily life (see also 1 John 3:16-18)?

_____

_____

_____

_____

_____

_____

_____

_____

_____

_____

_____

"In the Old Testament both Abraham (2 Chron. 20:7; Isa. 41:8; cf. Jas. 2:23) and Moses (Ex. 33:11) are called friends of God. This title is unusual and speaks of the highest relationship possible between God and a human being."[2]

10. How do you respond to the idea that Jesus not only loves (see verse 9) but also chose you (see verse 16) and considers you His friend (see verse 14)?

_____

_____

_____

_____

_____

_____

_____

_____

_____

_____

_____

11. What does Jesus' statement that He is the vine indicate to us about our ongoing connection to Him?

_____

_____

_____

_____

_____

_____

_____

_____

_____

_____

_____

Your Response

As part of the True Vine, we experience pruning and bear fruit. What implications do those two realities have for your daily life?

_____

_____

_____

_____

_____

_____

_____

_____

_____

_____

_____

_____

_____

_____

_____

_____

_____

_____

_____

_____

_____

_____

_____

For Further Study

Read Galatians 5:13-26. What kind of fruit does Jesus want to see in your life?

_____

_____

_____

_____

_____

_____

_____

_____

_____

_____

_____

_____

_____

_____

_____

_____

_____

_____

_____

_____

_____

_____

BEFORE ABRAHAM WAS, I AM

John 8:48-59

THOSE WHO SAY THAT JESUS was merely a great teacher or a wonderful moral example are often surprised to learn that He claimed to be God. The Jewish leaders in Jesus' day were equally astonished. They expected God to send the Messiah to save Israel, but they never imagined that the Messiah would be God Himself!

In John 8, Jesus and the Pharisees have an intense exchange, with each side challenging the other about whether God is their Father. The Pharisees also scoff at the extraordinary things Jesus is saying about who He is and why He has come. But even those series of disputes do not infuriate them as much as His final, extraordinary claim: "Before Abraham was born, I am" (verse 58).

---

1. Read John 8:48-59. What are the main points of dispute between Jesus and the Pharisees?

_____

_____

_____

_____

_____

_____

_____

_____

2. Which of Jesus' statements would you expect to offend the Pharisees?

_____

_____

_____

_____

_____

_____

_____

_____

_____

_____

_____

Andreas Köstenberger writes: "Calling Jesus a Samaritan may intimate that Jesus' miracles are due to demonic influence or magic. In a talmudic passage, a person who learned Scripture and the Mishnah but did not study with a rabbi is described by one teacher as belonging to 'the people of the land,' by another as a Samaritan, and by a third as a magician. Probably, the present insult is grounded in a whole cluster of ideas."[1]

3. Jesus had previously told the Jews that they were slaves to sin (see verse 34) and children of the devil (see verse 44). How did they intend to dishonor Jesus with their response (see verse 48; see also Mark 3:22-29)?

_____

_____

_____

_____

_____

_____

_____

_____

_____

_____

4. How do Jesus' other "I am" statements deepen the meaning of His words, "Very truly I tell you, whoever obeys my word will never see death" (verse 51)?

_____

_____

_____

_____

_____

_____

_____

_____

_____

_____

5. How do those in the crowd misunderstand and dispute what Jesus is saying (see verses 52-53)?

_____

_____

_____

_____

_____

_____

_____

_____

_____

_____

_____

"The OT Scriptures, Jewish tradition, and Greco-Roman beliefs agree that death is the common lot of humanity. 'What man can live and not see death, or save himself from the power of the grave?' writes the psalmist (Ps. 89:48). 'Where are your forefathers now? And the prophets, do they live forever?' asks the prophet (Zech. 1:5). Even people whom the Jews believed to have been exceptionally close to God were not exempt from death."[2]

Gary Burge writes: "Many rabbis in this period taught that Abraham possessed tremendous gifts of prophetic insight. God had given to him the secrets of the coming ages, which included an awareness of the coming Messiah. Even his 'rejoicing' at the birth of his son Isaac (Gen. 17:17; 21:6) was a foreshadowing of the blessing that would come to the world through his lineage. No rabbi would object to Jesus' claim that Abraham would see the messianic era. But Jesus does not say this. Instead, he says: 'Your father Abraham rejoiced at the thought of seeing *my day*; he saw it and was glad'. The messianic era is now fulfilled in Christ."[3]

6. Jesus refuses to "glorify" Himself (verse 54). What does it mean to "glorify" someone, and how do both God and Abraham glorify Jesus (see verses 54-56)?

_____

_____

_____

_____

_____

_____

_____

_____

_____

_____

7. Read Exodus 3:13-14. What do you think God means when he tells Moses that his name is "I AM WHO I AM" or simply "I AM"?

_____

_____

_____

_____

_____

_____

_____

_____

_____

_____

8. Jesus tells his hearers, "Very truly I tell you, . . . before Abraham was born, I am!" (verse 58). Why do you think this claim was so shocking to the Jews?

_____

_____

_____

_____

What evidence is there that those who heard Jesus understood exactly what he was claiming (see verse 59)?

_____

_____

_____

_____

_____

9. Why is Jesus' claim to be "I am"—the same God who spoke to Abraham—still surprising to many people today?

_____

_____

_____

_____

_____

_____

_____

_____

_____

_____

Leon Morris explains: "The Jews could interpret this as nothing other than blasphemy. Therefore they took up stones to stone him, this being the proper punishment for that offence (Lev. 24:16). In their angry state they felt that there was no other course. . . . So they took the law into their own hands."[4]

10. Taking each of Jesus' "I am" statements in the book of John (listed below), what do we know about Him?

I am . . .

the Bread of Life

_____

_____

_____

_____

_____

_____

_____

_____

the Light of the World

_____

_____

_____

_____

_____

_____

_____

_____

_____

_____

the Gate for the sheep

_____

_____

_____

_____

_____

_____

_____

_____

_____

the Good Shepherd

_____

_____

_____

_____

_____

_____

_____

_____

_____

_____

_____

the Resurrection and the Life

_____

_____

_____

_____

_____

_____

_____

_____

_____

_____

_____

_____

the True Vine

_____

_____

_____

_____

_____

_____

_____

_____

_____

_____

_____

_____

_____

the Way, the Truth, and the Life

_____

_____

_____

_____

_____

_____

_____

_____

_____

_____

_____

Before Abraham

_____

_____

_____

_____

_____

_____

_____

_____

_____

_____

_____

_____

11. How should the reality of who Jesus is—far more than just a great teacher, a prophet, or a moral example—affect our everyday lives?

_____

_____

_____

_____

_____

_____

_____

_____

_____

_____

Your Response

How can you "glorify" Jesus this week through your thoughts, actions, and worship?

_____

_____

_____

_____

_____

_____

_____

_____

_____

_____

For Further Study

Read the first chapter of John's Gospel. How do
John's words further clarify Jesus' divinity?

_____

_____

_____

_____

_____

_____

_____

_____

_____

_____

_____

_____

_____

_____

_____

_____

_____

_____

_____

_____

_____

_____

_____

_____

_____

NOTES

INTRODUCTION
1. Kyle Dillon, "Refuting 5 False Theories About Jesus," Gospel Coalition, October 12, 2015, https://www.thegospelcoalition.org/article/refuting-5-false-theories -about-jesus/.

SESSION ONE–I AM THE BREAD OF LIFE
1. Gary M. Burge, *John: The NIV Application Commentary*, ed. Terry Muck (Grand Rapids, MI: Zondervan, 2000), 197.
2. Burge, *John*, 198–99.
3. Burge, *John*, 201.

SESSION TWO–I AM THE LIGHT OF THE WORLD
1. Katie Kerwin McCrimmon, "Blind Woman Gets Her Sight Back," UCHealth, February 22, 2021, https://www.uchealth.org/today/blind-woman-gets-her -sight-back/.
2. *Holman Bible Dictionary*, s.v. "Blindness," accessed December 7, 2021, https://www .studylight.org/dictionaries/eng/hbd/b/blindness.html.
3. D. A. Carson, *The Gospel According to John*, Pillar New Testament Commentary (Grand Rapids, MI: Eerdmans, 1991), 361.
4. Gary M. Burge, *John: The NIV Application Commentary*, ed. Terry Muck (Grand Rapids, MI: Zondervan, 2000), 275.

SESSION THREE–I AM THE GATE FOR THE SHEEP
1. Taken from Jack Kuhatschek, *I Am the Way* (Grand Rapids, MI: Our Daily Bread, 2018). Reprinted by permission. All rights reserved.
2. D. A. Carson, *The Gospel According to John, Pillar New Testament Commentary* (Grand Rapids, MI: Eerdmans, 1991), 381.
3. Carson, *Gospel According to John*, 383.
4. Carson, *Gospel According to John*, 383.

SESSION FOUR–I AM THE GOOD SHEPHERD
1. Gary M. Burge, *John: The NIV Application Commentary*, ed. Terry Muck (Grand Rapids, MI: Zondervan, 2000), 290–91.

2. D. A. Carson, *The Gospel According to John, Pillar New Testament Commentary* (Grand Rapids, MI: Eerdmans, 1991), 386.

3. Steve Chalke and Alan Mann, *The Lost Message of Jesus* (Grand Rapids, MI: Zondervan, 2003), 182.

4. Burge, *John*, 291–92.

5. Carson, *Gospel According to John*, 388.

SESSION FIVE—I AM THE RESURRECTION AND THE LIFE

1. "D. L. Moody: More Alive than Ever," accessed December 8, 2021, https://www .crossroad.to/Quotes/faith/moody.htm.

2. Gary M. Burge, *John: The NIV Application Commentary*, ed. Terry Muck (Grand Rapids, MI: Zondervan, 2000), 315.

3. Burge, *John*, 316.

4. Blue Letter Bible, "Lexicon: Strong's G386—*anastasis*," accessed December 9, 2021, https://www.blueletterbible.org/lexicon/g386/niv/tr/0-1/.

5. Bible Hub, "Strong's 2222. *zóé*," accessed December 9, 2021, https://biblehub.com /greek/2222.htm.

SESSION SIX—I AM THE WAY, THE TRUTH, AND THE LIFE

1. Taken from Jack Kuhatschek, *I am the Way* (Grand Rapids, MI: Our Daily Bread, 2018). Reprinted by permission. All rights reserved. Boteach quote is from Larry King Live, "Should Christians Stop Trying to Convert Jews?" January 12, 2000, http://www.cnn .com/TRANSCRIPTS/0001/12/lkl.00.html.

2. D. A. Carson, *The Gospel According to John, Pillar New Testament Commentary* (Grand Rapids, MI: Eerdmans, 1991), 488–89.

3. Taken from Jack Kuhatschek, *I am the Way* (Grand Rapids, MI: Our Daily Bread, 2018). Reprinted by permission. All rights reserved.

4. Gary M. Burge, *John: The NIV Application Commentary*, ed. Terry Muck (Grand Rapids, MI: Zondervan, 2000), 60–61.

5. Leon Morris, *The Gospel According to John* (Grand Rapids, MI: Eerdmans, 1971), 646.

6. As quoted in Carson, *Gospel According to John*, 492.

SESSION SEVEN—I AM THE TRUE VINE

1. Andreas J. Köstenberger, *John: Baker Exegetical Commentary on the New Testament* (Grand Rapids, MI: Baker Academic, 2004), 450.

2. Gary M. Burge, *John: The NIV Application Commentary*, ed. Terry Muck (Grand Rapids, MI: Zondervan, 2000), 419.

SESSION EIGHT—BEFORE ABRAHAM WAS, I AM

1. Andreas J. Köstenberger, *John: Baker Exegetical Commentary on the New Testament* (Grand Rapids, MI: Baker Academic, 2004), 268–69.

2. Köstenberger, *John*, 270.

3. Gary M. Burge, *John: The NIV Application Commentary*, ed. Terry Muck (Grand Rapids, MI: Zondervan, 2000), 263.

4. Leon Morris, *The Gospel According to John* (Grand Rapids, MI: Eerdmans, 1971), 474.

LifeChange

A NAVPRESS BIBLE STUDY SERIES

LifeChange Bible studies train you in good Bible study practices even as you enjoy a robust and engaging Bible study experience. Learn the skill as you study the Word. There is a study for every book of the Bible and relevant topics.

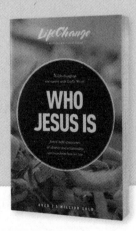

SINGLE COPIES AND BULK DISCOUNTS AT NAVPRESS.COM